Disasters *in* Nature

Hurricanes

Catherine Chambers

Heinemann Library
Chicago, Illinois

Customer Service 888-454-2279

Visit our website at www.heinemannlibrary.com

Designed by Celia Floyd
Originated by Dot Gradations
Printed by Wing King Tong in Hong Kong

05 04 03 02
10 9 8 7 6 5 4 3 2

Library of Congress Cataloging-in-Publication Data
Chambers, Catherine, 1954-
    Hurricanes / Catherine Chambers.
       p. cm. — (Disasters in nature)
    Includes bibliographical references and index.
    Summary: Examines hurrcanes, discussing how they are formed, how they are tracked, and what kinds of damage they can cause. Includes a section on 1998's Hurricane Georges.
    ISBN 1-57572-429-4 (lib. bdg.)   ISBN 1-58810-334-X (pbk. bdg.)
    1. Hurricanes—Juvenile literature. [1. Hurricanes.] I. Title.
QC944.2.C48 2000
551.55'2—dc21   00-020023

Acknowledgments

The Publishers would like to thank the following for permission to reproduce photographs:

Planet Earth Pictures, p. 6; FLPA/D. Hoadley, p. 8; Panos/Pedro Guzman, p. 9; Pictor, pp. 10, 37; Colorific/Cindy Karp, p. 11; FLPA/Roger Wilmshurst, p. 12; Hulton Getty, p. 13; BBC Natural History Unit/Mike Wilkes, p. 15; Planet Earth Pictures/Rosemary Calvert, p. 19; BBC Natural History Unit/M. W. Richards, p. 21; Photri, pp. 23, 31; FLPA/M. Nimmo, p. 25; NHPA/Alan Williams, p. 25; FLPA/Robert Steinau, p. 27; Still Pictures/Gil Moti, p. 32; Colorific/Lori Grinker/Contact, p. 33; NHPA/A.N.T., p. 34; Panos/Neil Cooper, p. 35; Katz Pictures, p. 36; Corbis, p. 38; NHPA/Kevin Schafer, p. 40; Still Pictures/Norbert Wu, p. 41; BBC Natural History Unit/Michael & Patricia Fogden, p. 42; FLPA/Jurgen & Christine Sohns, p. 43; Ardea/Richard Vaughan, p. 45.

Cover photograph reproduced with permission of Robert Harding Picture Library.

Our thanks to Professor Ed Brotak of the University of North Carolina—Asheville for his comments in the preparation of this book.

Some words are shown in bold, **like this.** You can find out what they mean by looking in the glossary.

Contents

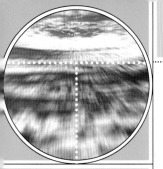

What Is a Hurricane?

A **hurricane** is a powerful storm that sweeps in from the ocean, causing destruction wherever it hits land. Technically, these frightening storms are **tropical cyclones**—fierce, inward-whirling storms with winds that rage at a speed of at least 75 miles (120 kilometers) per hour. The winds blow in an inward spiral from an area of **high pressure** to an area of **low pressure.**

Where do hurricanes happen?

Hurricane-force winds can happen anywhere in the world, but true hurricanes are tropical storms. They begin over tropical waters, often in the mid-Atlantic and Pacific Oceans. They hit the Caribbean Islands and the east coast of the United States on one side of the world, and India, Japan, the Far East, and Northern Australia on the other.

Hurricane highlights

The technical name for a hurricane is a tropical cyclone. There are other names, too, that come from the languages of people who live in hurricane disaster zones in different parts of the world.

Hurricane is the name given to tropical cyclones that hit the Caribbean Islands, the coast of Central America, and the east coast of the United States. The word was first used by the Taino people of the Caribbean Islands.

Typhoon is the name for tropical cyclones that hit China, Japan, and other lands in the China Sea and the western Pacific.

Tropical cyclone is the name used for these fierce rotating storms when they affect India and Australia.

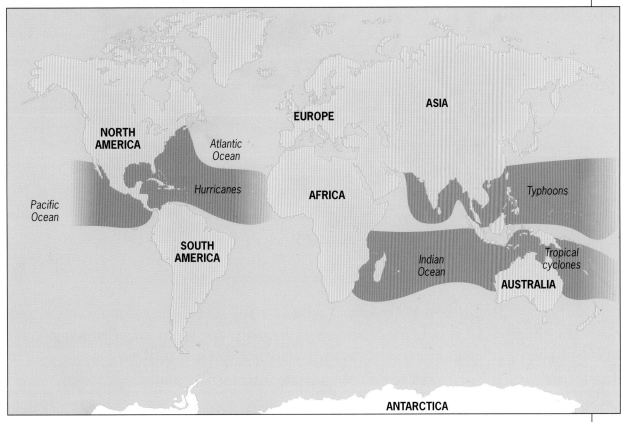

This map shows the main hurricane zones.

Hurricanes in our hands

To many people, it seems as though the strength and frequency of hurricanes have increased in the last 30 years. They point to **global warming** and the **El Niño** effect as possible reasons for this change. However, most **meteorologists** agree that hurricanes have not actually increased. What has increased is the damage they cause—more people than ever before are building homes and businesses in hurricane danger zones.

Hurricanes on our minds

In addition to hurricanes causing more damage, we also hear more about them. Through satellite communications, television, newspapers, and the Internet, homes throughout the world can see and listen to the devastation caused by natural disasters.

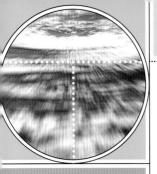

The Trail of Hurricane Georges

Tracking Georges

The first hint of a **hurricane** on the Atlantic coast of the U.S. begins right across the ocean in West Africa. It was here, on September 13, 1998, that a satellite image picked up the beginnings of a storm system. As warm, damp air met with the cold **easterly jet,** the moisture condensed and formed towering clouds.

On September 15, ships in the area noted the first signs that a hurricane was forming. An area of very **low pressure** with winds rushing into it was observed south of the Cape Verde Islands. On September 16, the cloud and wind system became a tropical storm—the first stage of a hurricane. For ten days it swept across the ocean, along a well-worn northwest track towards the Caribbean Sea. By the afternoon of September 19, U.S. Air Force Reserve aircraft were measuring the winds and the central air pressure of the system. Satellite information confirmed that the hurricane was getting stronger. Later that day, a hurricane with strength of Force 4 on the **Saffir-Simpson hurricane scale** was measured. By September 20, east of the Lesser Antilles Islands, the hurricane reached its peak.

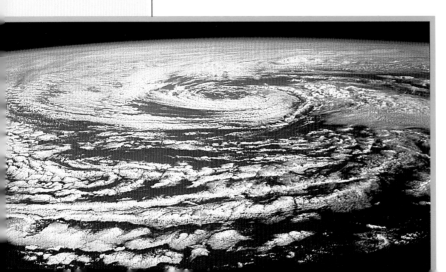

To the north of the equator, hurricane winds blow into a central "hole" called an eye, in a counterclockwise direction. South of the equator, they blow clockwise.

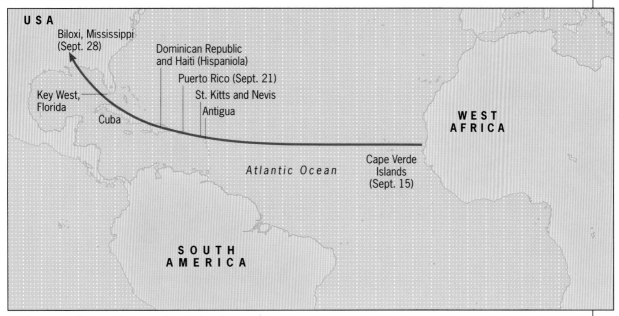

This map charts the track of Hurricane Georges, in September 1998.

Landfall!

Landfall occurred first on the island of Antigua. When the hurricane hit Hispaniola, the island that is home to Haiti and the Dominican Republic, the clouds rose over the mountains and cooled. The **water vapor** they held **condensed** into droplets that fell as heavy rain. **Flash floods** and deadly mudslides followed. From Hispaniola the hurricane moved over Cuba and towards the United States. Here, it first hit Key West, Florida, and slowed down as it moved northwest on September 26–27. It next made landfall on September 28, near Biloxi, Mississippi, and then swirled around the southern Mississippi River, dying down all the time. By October 1, it was all over.

In total, Hurricane Georges hit seven areas in the Caribbean Islands and the United States between September 15 and October 1, 1998. It caused 602 deaths, as well as damage costing billions of dollars.

After Hurricane Georges

Scientists are still measuring the exact impact of **Hurricane** Georges. They will be examining the complicated **meteorological** and oceanographic data for a long time to come. Most of the data concerns the United States and the Caribbean.

Storm surge statistics

Hurricanes can cause **storm surges** as they hit the coast. Storm surges are huge walls of water that are formed when the strong winds that form a hurricane push the water along. They are very destructive and cause more deaths than any other hurricane feature.

So far, the heights of storm surges caused by Hurricane Georges have only been estimated. On the island of Puerto Rico, they reached about 10 feet (3 meters) and on the United States mainland they reached between 5 and 12 feet (1.5-3.7 meters). Waves breaking over the top of a storm surge can increase its height, but this is very difficult to measure accurately.

Once a hurricane hits land, it can cause tornadoes to form. Hurricane Georges was accompanied by 28 tornadoes, mostly in Alabama and Florida, although two struck in Puerto Rico.

Rain and flood

One of the worst features of Hurricane Georges was torrential rainfall. Over two days, Puerto Rico received 25 inches (625 millimeters), while 30 inches (753 millimeters) fell on Bay Minette in Alabama. Southern Mississippi faced flood disaster from September 30 to October 2, when floodwaters forced many people to **evacuate** their homes.

Counting the cost

It is estimated that on Puerto Rico 72,605 homes were damaged, with 28,005 completely destroyed. On the island of Hispaniola, the Dominican Republic was left with 185,000 people homeless and on the other half of the island, in Haiti, 167,332 people lost their homes. Many of them remained in temporary housing for several weeks until electricity and water supplies were restored. But on the mainland of the United States, only 1,536 homes were damaged in Florida, 173 of which were completely destroyed—mostly mobile homes and trailers.

The American Red Cross mounted a huge relief operation in the United States and the islands hit by Hurricane Georges. It became the most expensive relief effort in the organization's 117-year history. In all, the cost of Hurricane Georges has so far been estimated at $5.9 billion.

Flash flooding and mudslides on the hillsides of the Dominican Republic and Haiti caused most of the deaths in this particular hurricane disaster.

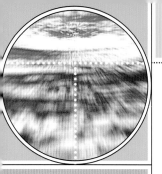

Hitting the Headlines

Hurricane Georges soon made headlines in the United States and throughout the world. National newspapers, television, and radio news bulletins give a lot of important information in the days when a hurricane is approaching. These media can reach millions of people in the affected areas, who are anxiously waiting for an overall picture of what could happen. National and local Internet websites can track a hurricane on a daily and even hourly basis, giving detailed up-to-date weather information, **evacuation** instructions, and advice to people living in the hurricane's path.

Rich and poor

The United States has **invested** a lot of money in modern hurricane tracking systems, as well as evacuation programs. The most important part of such programs is making sure that people have access to the information. Weather stations have linked up with radio and television newsrooms, which interrupt programs if a hurricane is on the way.

The first detailed reports of hurricane disasters in developing countries usually come after the event, when foreign aid agencies and reporters start moving in to assess the damage. Compare this to the huge amount of information that is given out if a similar disaster occurs in a richer country.

When power lines snap, bridges break, and roads are blocked, it means that news coverage of hurricanes is made even more difficult. Journalists who cannot get to the disaster zone can only report government statistics and information issued by aid agencies.

Too much news?

There is more news coverage on hurricanes than ever before, with increasingly detailed accounts of the paths they take and the damage they cause. With modern technology, we are able to monitor them in more detail and broadcast their effects over a wider area. All this information might lead us to believe that the world's climatic disasters are taking a turn for the worse. Although many weather patterns have changed in recent years, hurricanes have remained relatively steady. It is the damage they cause that has increased, as more people live in hurricane zones than ever before.

Meteorologists at the U.S. National Hurricane Center monitor storm movement and development. They use satellite and radar information to track hurricanes and to prepare hurricane warnings.

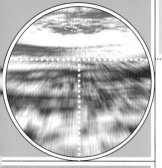

The Hurricane Zones

The map on page 5 shows that most **hurricane** zones are in the hotter part of the world. These areas, the Tropics, border the equator, where the heat from the sun beats down almost directly.

The heat absorbed by the land or sea at any place in the world depends on the angle at which the sun's rays reach the earth at that point. This gives the earth its different climatic zones. At the equator, where the sun's heat beats down from directly overhead, the climate is hotter. Towards the poles, the sun's heat hits the earth at an angle, leading to a cooler climate. The strong heating effect around the equator is the main reason for the movement of air masses around the earth. The warm, **equatorial** air rises up to the **tropopause,** where the air is thinner and colder, and air from surrounding areas comes in to replace it. Having risen to the high point, air masses disperse, making their way towards the poles, where they help to create weather systems.

Even places as unlikely as England can occasionally be hit by hurricanes when an Atlantic hurricane turns northward.

Where and when?

Hurricane zones lie in the tropics, where the sea is warm—especially when the sun is directly overhead. Then, the temperature rarely falls below 79° F (26° C). Warm, moist air rises from the warm sea, often leading to a hurricane.

The largest hurricane zones are on the western sides of oceans. Deep layers of warm, moist air collect there and fuel the hurricanes as they move westward.

Many hurricanes begin as waves of air coming from the east, high up in the **Intertropical Convergence Zone,** which lies around the equator. Air is greatly heated, rises, is dispersed, then gets pulled back towards the equator again, helped by the earth's rotation. This circular movement often contributes to the start of a tropical storm system or a hurricane.

Not all hurricanes occur on the west coasts of the oceans. Many hit the northeast and northwest coasts of India. These particular hurricanes, called **tropical cyclones,** are caused by a change in the **monsoon winds.** These winds blow across the land towards the southwest in winter, but turn and blow northwards across the ocean in summer from about May to September. The warm seas often give rise to fierce cyclones that devastate the coasts of Bangladesh and northern India.

In Australia, in 1974, **flash floods** were so bad that the northern city of Darwin was **evacuated.** Water rose to the tops of telegraph poles. Hundreds of thousands of sheep drowned on the flooded pastures.

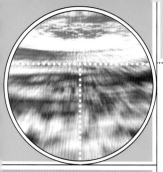

Rain and Wind

Rain is a feature of **hurricanes,** and when it is heavy enough, it can cause serious flooding. It is part of the **water cycle.** This describes the way in which the earth's supply of water is recycled all the time in different forms. Sometimes it is held in the air as invisible **water vapor** or in clouds as tiny droplets. Sometimes it falls as rain, sleet, snow, or hail. But most of it lies in massive oceans, seas, lakes, and rivers, or it is frozen in ice sheets and glaciers. The water cycle is a global system that changes very quickly, so it is very difficult to predict perfectly.

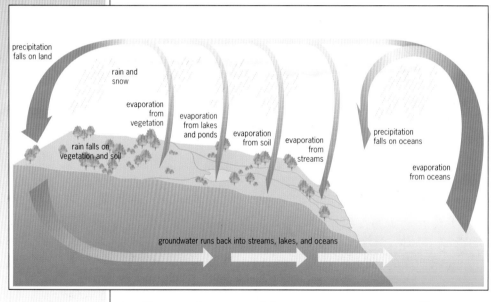

precipitation falls on land

rain and snow

evaporation from vegetation

evaporation from lakes and ponds

evaporation from soil

evaporation from streams

precipitation falls on oceans

evaporation from oceans

rain falls on vegetation and soil

groundwater runs back into streams, lakes, and oceans

The amount of moisture that is **evaporated** into the air by the heat of the sun affects the size and number of the clouds.

Why does the rain fall?

When the sun shines and the wind blows over the oceans and other large water masses, it heats the water so much that some evaporates. If the air above the water is warm it holds a lot of vapor—warm air can hold more moisture than cold air. Warm air is also less dense than cold air because heat makes the **molecules** move further apart. So the warm air rises, carrying the water vapor with it. As the warm, moist air rises, it cools and **condenses** into tiny droplets that form clouds.

When the clouds grow even higher, the **super-cooled** icy droplets become larger and heavier as even more water vapor condenses. Eventually these droplets are too heavy to stay in the cloud, so they fall as rain. Some rain falls on the oceans, but a lot falls on land. Clouds rise up hills and mountain slopes, cooling and shedding rain before they reach the other side. The drops fall down the slopes, gathering in tiny streams. The streams flow into rivers, and the rivers into seas. And so the cycle begins all over again.

What makes the wind blow?

Wind is caused by air moving from areas of **high pressure** to areas of **low pressure.** This exchange of air masses can be quite gentle—just a faint breeze might blow. But if there is an area of very low pressure, caused by a lot of warm air rising, then air from the high pressure area rushes in fast, in the form of winds, to fill the space. This rush of wind is what makes a hurricane so strong.

This dark, towering, **cumulonimbus** cloud is the type of cloud that can develop into a hurricane as it sweeps across warm seas. **Tornadoes,** too, come from this type of cloud, from bulges that hang down at the bottom.

What Makes a Hurricane?

Under pressure

Many **hurricanes** develop where winds meet in the tropics, usually between mid-May and November. Hurricanes form when great masses of very warm and very moist air rise. The rising air causes areas of very **low pressure** that form the center around which the warm air rises in a whirling, upward spiral. As it does so, cooler air from an area of **high pressure** rushes into the space it has left at its base.

The rising air cools as it rises. The moisture in the air **condenses,** forming banks of very heavy, low-lying, rain-bearing clouds. The continual formation of clouds and thunderstorms also releases heat into the air, which fuels the whirling hurricane even more. The upward-turning spiral and the downward-rushing air move faster and faster as they approach land, and the sea provides very little resistance to it. Not all hurricanes move over land—many die out at sea. If a hurricane reaches land, it begins to run out of "fuel"—there is no more warm moisture to pick up. There is also more friction with land and vegetation than there is with water. This friction slows the wind and the hurricane gradually dies, but in many cases the damage has already been done.

The map shows that the main winds in the Tropics curl towards the equator.

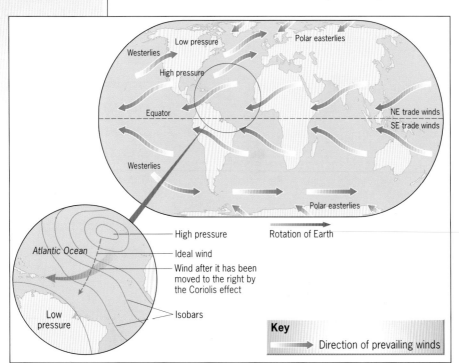

Low pressure

Westerlies

High pressure

Equator

Westerlies

Polar easterlies

NE trade winds
SE trade winds

Polar easterlies

Rotation of Earth

Atlantic Ocean

High pressure

Ideal wind

Wind after it has been moved to the right by the Coriolis effect

Isobars

Low pressure

Key

Direction of prevailing winds

What helps a hurricane spin?

If air moved in a simple, straight direction from high pressure to low pressure, then hurricanes might not happen at all. But as the earth rotates from west to east, air movement is shifted slightly. North of the **equator** it moves to the right, and to the south it moves to the left. This is caused by the **Coriolis force.** At the equator, the Coriolis force is zero, and no hurricanes form there, but it the surrounding areas it is strong enough to start them forming.

The eye of the storm

The eye is formed when a hurricane reaches its peak. It is a wide column of calm, descending air right in the middle of the cylinder of warm, rising air that is wrapped around it. This tube of dry air, surrounded by walls of clouds, reaches up to a clear, blue, sunny sky.

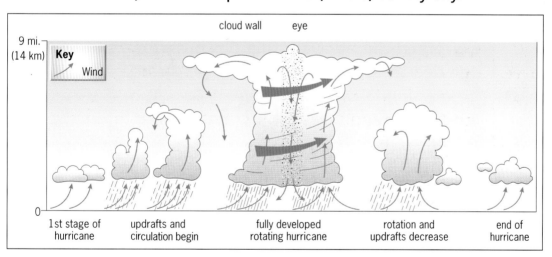

When a hurricane begins to develop, the contrasts in temperatures and air pressure within the hurricane help to increase its power.

The Effects of El Niño

In recent years **El Niño** has been one of the most talked-about causes of freak natural disasters in the world. This phenomenon creates great extremes, from violent **hurricanes** and terrifying twisters, torrential rain and heavy flooding, to severe drought, dust storms, and forest fires. It also makes predicting and coping with natural disasters almost impossible. There is a similar phenomenon in the atmosphere above the Atlantic Ocean. This change in **air pressure** and winds is known as the North Atlantic Oscillation (NAO). It affects western Europe and North Africa.

El Niño was first noticed by anchovy fishermen off the coast of Peru. Every few years the cold coastal waters and the air above them warmed up, causing more moisture to be **evaporated** into the air. This brought welcome rain to the dry shores of Peru around Christmas time. Over the years, however, this mild, welcomed climatic variation has brought a series of dreaded disasters.

The power of El Niño

El Niño is a very strange and complex climatic feature, affecting both the northern and southern **hemispheres** of the earth, as well as the two largest oceans. It begins in the Pacific Ocean as a sudden reversal of the prevailing winds, which normally blow in a predictable east-west direction all year. These changing winds blow towards the coast of South America, warming up the water and the air as they go. This combination of warm water and air can create storm clouds and violent hurricane-force winds.

Neither of these dramatic changes in the atmosphere acts on its own. Changes in the oceans' powerful currents can affect the weather patterns above. In addition, many scientists believe that **global warming** plays a part in El Niño.

We can discover a lot about past climate patterns—including El Niños—by studying tree rings. Each ring in a tree's trunk represents one year's growth. When the ring is narrow, it means that the tree has not grown very fast. It has either not had enough moisture or enough sunlight. We can also learn about past climates by studying soil sediments at the bottom of the ocean, thick ice at the poles, and coral reefs.

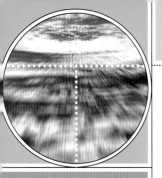

Global Warming—and More Hurricanes?

Most scientists agree that the world's climate is getting warmer. We know now that it takes a difference of only 2-4° F (1-2° C) to change the earth's climate and weather patterns quite dramatically. Many scientists predict that in 30 years the earth will be at least 1.8° F (1° C) warmer than it is now.

Living in a greenhouse

Most people agree that the **greenhouse effect** is partly responsible for **global warming.** It is caused by gases such as **carbon dioxide** rising into the **atmosphere.** Normally, when heat from the sun reaches the earth, some is absorbed and some is reflected and **radiated** back. But the greenhouse gases in the atmosphere trap the sun's heat, warming the earth.

A large percentage of greenhouse gases are produced by burning fossil fuels such as coal and oil in power stations, factories, and homes throughout the world. Switching to alternate energy sources, such as solar or wind power, could help slow—and maybe even begin to reverse—the greenhouse effect.

If the earth's temperature rises too much, frozen tundra lands, such as those of Siberia in Russia, will start to thaw. This will release **methane** gases from decayed plant matter trapped underneath the ice, increasing the greenhouse effect even more.

A hole in the sky

The earth is surrounded by a layer of gases known as the atmosphere that keeps the full strength of the sun from reaching the earth. The atmosphere also filters out harmful **ultra-violet rays.** One of the most effective protective gases is **ozone,** which forms a layer in the **stratosphere.** In recent years, the layer of ozone has thinned, especially over Antarctica. This has led to increased **radiation** from the sun, causing increased health risks from the ultra-violet radiation.

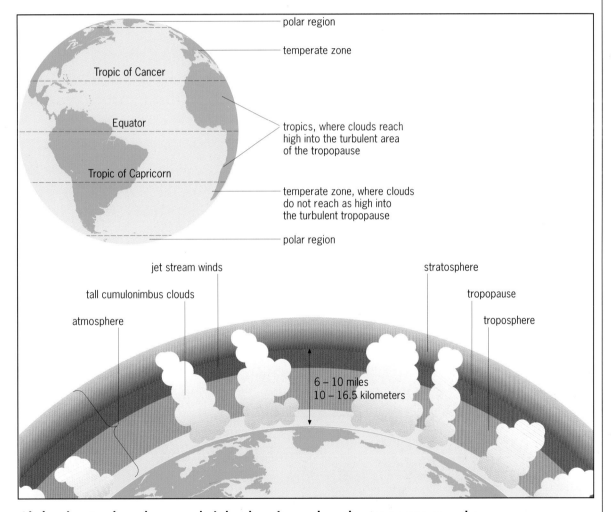

polar region

temperate zone

Tropic of Cancer

Equator

tropics, where clouds reach high into the turbulent area of the tropopause

Tropic of Capricorn

temperate zone, where clouds do not reach as high into the turbulent tropopause

polar region

jet stream winds

stratosphere

tall cumulonimbus clouds

tropopause

atmosphere

troposphere

6 – 10 miles
10 – 16.5 kilometers

Air begins to slow down and sink when it reaches the **tropopause**—the layer between the **troposphere** and the stratosphere. There is more **turbulence** in the tropical tropopause than in other parts of the layer. This is why weather phenomena such as **hurricanes** and **tornadoes** occur so often near the equator.

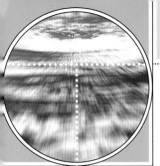

The Hurricane Hits!

Destructive Force

What happens when a **hurricane** hits land? There are four main destructive forces: high wind, heavy rain, storm surges, and sliding mud. Together they can kill humans and animals, destroy buildings, bridges, roads, and railroads, and devastate crops. The wind alone can snap mature trees in half and even bend and break steel structures. The table below shows what happens when hurricanes of different forces hit the land. It is known as the **Saffir-Simpson hurricane scale.**

Status	Wind strength (knots)	Wind strength (mph)	Damage potential
Depression	up to 35	up to 38	
Tropical storm	35–64	38–73	
Category 1 Hurricane	65–83	74–95	Flooding of low-lying areas, flying debris, and fallen trees. Homes not tied down suffer the most damage, especially mobile homes. Fishing piers may suffer damage.
Category 2 Hurricane	84–95	96–110	There is significant damage to mobile homes, vegetation, and piers. There is a little damage to doors, roofing materials, and windows on buildings.
Category 3 Hurricane	96–113	111–130	Mobile homes are destroyed. Some damage to homes and buildings. Coastal homes and buildings are flooded.
Category 4 Hurricane	114–134	131–155	Homes and buildings are severely damaged or destroyed. Major flooding occurs along the coastline and inland.
Category 5 Hurricane	135 or more	156 or more	Homes and buildings are completely destroyed. Severe flooding occurs well inland.

Fear of flood

Flooding can be the most dangerous result of a hurricane. This is especially so in large **delta** areas such as the coast of Bangladesh, where the Brahmaputra and Ganges Rivers meet the sea. Rain sweeps inland with the **tropical cyclone** and swells the rivers so that the flow of water through the **floodplain** and coastal delta are greatly increased. Flooding can be even worse if a **storm surge** flows in from the sea. Flooding can also occur further inland, as the hurricane winds drive the clouds away from the sea towards cooler, drier air.

Flowing mud

On bare slopes, torrential rain can combine with loose earth and gravel to form a heavy mass of mud, which slides to the bottom of the slope by the action of gravity. Mudslides are common features when hurricanes hit areas where there has been large-scale **deforestation.** When the trees are gone, there is nothing to hold back the sliding mud.

In 1996, Hurricane Fran hit Washington, D.C. and the surrounding area. In just a few hours, 4 inches (102 millimeters) lashed down on the city streets. This picture from Alexandria, Virginia shows the scale of the flooding.

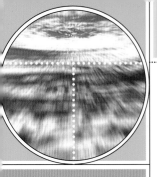

Walls of Water

A **storm surge** is one of the most feared outcomes of a **hurricane,** especially in the western Pacific and along the low-lying coasts of Bangladesh, Pakistan, and northwest India. A storm surge is created by the action of strong, hurricane-force winds blowing over the ocean. They pile up the water into a huge wall and drive it toward the shore. Some waves can reach a height of 30 feet (8 meters), causing severe coastal flooding. This is made worse by a general rise in sea level of up to 20 inches (50 centimeters).

Heavy rain on the sea and the coast, combined with a high tide, can make the situation even worse. It is very difficult to know how many deaths are caused by a storm surge on its own, but it is estimated that about 90 percent of deaths along a flooded coast are caused by drowning in these huge waves. **Global warming** has caused sea levels to rise slightly over the last 100 years, making floods more likely. As the earth's average temperature continues to rise, so do the oceans.

Hurricane highlights

The level of a storm surge depends on:

- the speed of the storm's forward motion

- the distance from the storm center to the eye wall

- the **air pressure** at the center of the eye—the lower it is, the faster the wind

- the steepness of the seafloor as it rises to the coast—and therefore the normal depths of water close to the shore

- the shape of the seafloor as it rises to the coast

- the angle of the storm as it hits the coast

The polder lands of the Netherlands are vast areas of farmland reclaimed from the sea. In February 1953 a massive storm surge caused by hurricane-force winds flooded the polders. Nearly 2,000 people were drowned, 72,000 were evacuated from their homes, and about 50,000 cattle died.

Storm surge stories

In 1938, 600 people were swept to their death by a storm surge as a hurricane hit Rhode Island. A wall of water 14 feet (4.3 meters) high swept through the streets. Nowadays, earlier warnings can be given so that people have more time to **evacuate.** Over the years, the population has increased so much that the death toll would be even worse if there was no time to escape.

In 1969, Hurricane Camille battered the coasts of Florida, Alabama, and Mississippi. A 27-foot (8.2-meter) storm surge, combined wih **flash floods,** killed over 200 people.

Storm surges are not just deadly—they are devastating. They sweep sand inland, covering coastal roads and **sandblasting** buildings, and they break harbor walls, roads, and bridges connecting islands. The salt water rots wooden structures and pollutes farmland.

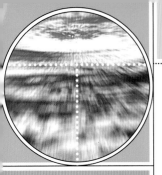

On the Edge of the Hurricane

Many **hurricanes** are made worse by violent, twisting, sucking winds that often whirl alongside them, mostly over land. These are known as **tornadoes**—fast winds that rotate around a funnel of very **low pressure.** They form inside deep **cumulonimbus** thunderclouds, and appear to hang from them in an upside-down cone.

A tornado's funnel may be quite narrow—no more than 330 feet (100 meters) across at its widest point—or it may be as much as a mile (1.6 kilometers). The tornado's path may be as short as a mile or two (a few kilometers) or it might run for over 450 miles (725 kilometers)!

The United States suffers more tornadoes than any other country in the world—often 1,000 or more in a year. The area of the United States most commonly hit by tornadoes is often called Tornado Alley. It runs from the Gulf of Mexico, through Oklahoma and Kansas, almost as far as the Great Lakes. Australia, Canada, parts of Russia, central Asia, Japan, and Italy are also tornado targets.

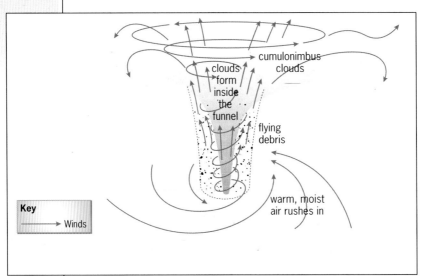

cumulonimbus clouds

clouds form inside the funnel

flying debris

warm, moist air rushes in

Key

→ Winds

Although we know how tornadoes form and spin, no one knows exactly why they appear.

How do tornadoes form?

Tornadoes often run in clusters to the right of incoming hurricanes, but they build up mostly over land, not over the sea. They need some of the same conditions as hurricanes in order to form and maintain their spin. They begin in an area of very low pressure and they need a layer of very warm, humid air near the ground that rises to meet a mass of cool, dry air very high above.

A horizontal wind blows continually at an angle caused by the **Coriolis force,** and the twisting motion begins. Air rushes in at the bottom to replace the warm, rising air, sucking air up faster through the funnel as it does so. Thunderclouds form inside the funnel as the lowest layer keeps warming up. They **condense** quite low down and release more heat, fueling the tornado.

Tracking the tornado

For over 20 years, scientists have tracked tornadoes using the **Doppler radar** system. The system sends out microwaves that are reflected by water droplets in the storm. Using this data, **meteorologists** can tell when a circular movement of wind is about to move out of it. Radar is especially important for tracking tornadoes that cannot be easily spotted—at night, or when they are wrapped in clouds or rain.

When tornadoes hit, they can suck up everything they touch—roofs, walls, cars, trees, telegraph poles, and people.

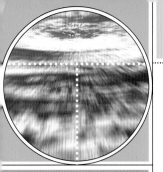

Tracking the Hurricane

The map on page 5 shows that **hurricanes** usually occur in the same parts of the world. Each year, they make their way in the usual direction along well-worn routes, but their **landfall** is not the same every time. Tracking a hurricane's exact path and predicting its landfall is therefore very important. So is assessing the width, strength, and duration of a hurricane, as well as the height of **storm surges** it causes and the amount and duration of rainfall. When scientists have this information, they can issue more accurate warnings.

Hurricane highlights

Specialists from different areas of science work together to predict hurricanes. **Meteorologists** study the climate and the atmosphere. **Oceanographers** look at the change in temperature and currents of the oceans. The following are some of the things they look for:

- Warm seas that are at temperatures of at least 79° F (about 26° C) down to a depth of 200 feet (60 meters) are perfect fuel for a hurricane.

- Deep, dark clouds and towering **cumulonimbus** clouds are typical signals of a hurricane and can be monitored using aircraft **radar** and satellite images.

- Hook-shaped clouds are the first definite signs that a hurricane is beginning its turning motion. As they grow and spin, they are monitored by **Doppler radar** and satellite.

- To estimate the height of a storm surge, oceanographers calculate wind speed, the **air pressure** on the sea, the speed of the storm, the position of the center of the hurricane, its size, the height of the tide, and the shape of the coastline. This gives them a good idea of how high the waters will rise.

Prediction problems

Computer models of previous hurricanes help predict when, where, and how fiercely a hurricane will hit land, but they can easily be inaccurate. Sometimes, a landfall can occur more than 60 miles (100 kilometers) from the predicted spot! Problems can arise when a hurricane hits islands and then continues over more sea before its final landfall on the mainland. The islands slow a hurricane down and often alter its course, and it is difficult to predict how much speed it will pick up again before it hits the next coastline.

Hurricanes can swerve as landfall occurs. This is partly due to the earth's spin pushing the winds off course— the **Coriolis force**—and partly due to the slowing down of the hurricane as it reaches the land.

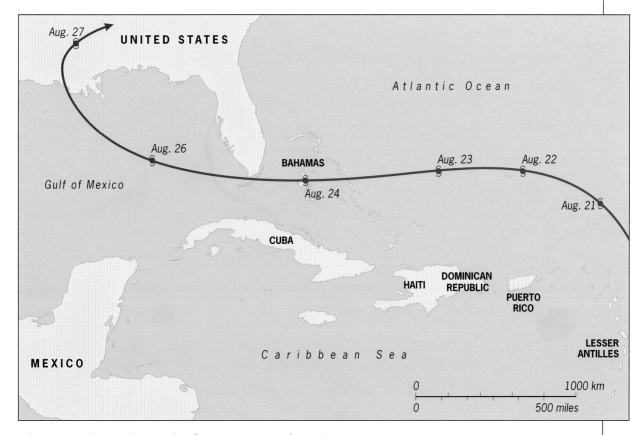

This map shows the path of Hurricane Andrew in 1992, illustrating how it swerved from a northwest direction to the northeast when it hit the mainland.

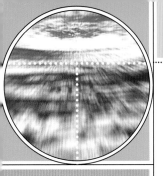

Hunting for Hurricanes

Meteorologists use information gathered by satellite, civilian and military aircraft, ships, air balloons, and coastal **radar** to monitor a **hurricane** as it makes its way across the ocean. When combined, these data give a detailed picture of the hurricane's size, shape, direction, turning speed, approach speed, moisture content, and cloud type.

Tracking Georges

This is just a small sample of all the information gathered and plotted every six hours as Hurricane Georges grew into a hurricane. Meteorologists tracked its latitude, longitude, and speed. We can see from the table when the storm changed from a tropical depression into a tropical storm and then into hurricane. In this table, wind speed has been measured in knots, or nautical miles per hour. One knot is the same as 1.151 miles (1.825 kilometers) per hour.

Date	Time	Latitude (north)	Longitude (west)	Pressure (millibars)	Wind speed (knots)	Stage
09/15	1200	9° 7′	25° 1′	1009	30	Tropical depression
09/15	1800	9° 8′	26° 5′	1009	30	Tropical depression
09/16	0000	10° 0′	28° 1′	1009	30	Tropical depression
09/16	0600	10° 3′	29° 7′	1009	30	Tropical depression
09/16	1200	10° 6′	31° 3′	1005	35	Tropical storm
09/16	1800	11° 0′	32° 9′	1003	35	Tropical storm
09/17	0000	11° 3′	34° 6′	1000	45	Tropical storm
09/17	0600	11° 7′	36° 3′	997	50	Tropical storm
09/17	1200	12° 0′	38° 1′	994	55	Tropical storm
09/17	1800	12° 3′	40° 0′	987	65	Hurricane

This tracking table continued until the hurricane died on October 1, 1998 at 6:00 A.M.

Hurricane hunters

In the United States, the Air Force Reserve actually fly aircraft into the eye of the hurricane! The aircraft are specially designed to withstand the high winds, and the flight crew are trained to navigate through the clouds and **turbulence** within the hurricane. They measure flight-level wind speeds and **air pressure** at the center of the storm.

Getting the picture

Doppler radar is used to estimate the shape of a hurricane and the circulation of wind. Doppler radar sends out a radio signal that is reflected by droplets of moisture in the hurricane back to the receiver. When several Doppler radars are used, a three-dimensional picture of cloud circulation is built up. This gives an idea of the wind speed and direction within the storm.

During Hurricane Georges, the Air Force Reserve and the National Oceanic and Atmospheric Administration flew a total of 23 missions to measure wind speed and pressure in the center of the hurricane. This hurricane spotter plane has a radar system in its nose.

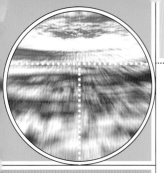

Hurricane Warning!

A problem of timing

The prediction of **hurricanes** must be matched by good warning systems, which most countries in the tropical hurricane zones have developed. A good warning will give people 24 hours to prepare for a hurricane, although it is not easy to say exactly where a hurricane will strike so far in advance. Huge numbers of people over wide areas therefore have to be warned, just in case the hurricane strikes. In the western Pacific, hundreds of tiny islands lie in the path of hurricanes. It is even more difficult here to predict the strength of the hurricane and give people proper warning. It is impossible to **evacuate** people on a very small island, so finding protective shelter in good time is the only answer.

Many big cities lie in the path of hurricanes. Here, evacuation is an enormous, costly undertaking, growing even bigger as urban populations increase. **Meteorologists** are under a lot of pressure to find ways of predicting hurricanes more accurately. This will lead to better preparation over smaller areas, saving lives and lowering costs. It takes about $200,000 to evacuate just one square mile (2.5 square kilometers) of a residential area.

Bangladesh has very up-to-date hurricane prediction systems, but the geography of Bangladesh makes it very difficult to know exactly how badly a hurricane will affect it. Most people live on the **floodplain**, or on sandbanks called chars near the wide river **estuaries.** When rain lashes down on the river estuary, water levels rise, which act with an incoming **storm surge** to create massive flooding.

Getting ready—keeping in touch

On the southeast coast of the United States, the first phase of the alert begins about 24 hours before a hurricane hits. This phase is known as a **hurricane watch.** Since it is uncertain where **landfall** will occur, there is no evacuation—people just make sure they keep updated by listening to the radio, watching television, or checking the Internet.

About six hours later, hurricane landfall predictions are more accurate. This is because the hurricane will be approaching coastal **radar** stations, which can help to calculate statistics more precisely. From this time onwards, specific warnings, called **hurricane warnings,** are issued in danger zones. This is when people begin to carry out their local evacuation plan.

Hurricane Gilbert struck the Caribbean Island of Jamaica on September 12, 1998. It was one of the worst hurricanes in the island's history. A quarter of all the houses were badly damaged or destroyed. Parts of the airport (above) were ruined and the planes were wrecked. But only 45 people died. This is because Jamaica has well-organized and well-publicized evacuation plans.

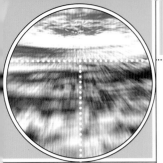

Preventing the Damage

Some of the poorest countries in the world are located in **hurricane** zones. Many people live in poor-quality housing right in the path of the winds. These homes are constructed of wood, plastic, and corrugated-iron sheeting—materials that break and blow away easily. In coastal areas, **storm surges** soak wooden structures with salt water, which eventually rots the wood. Even concrete foundations and walls eventually crumble if they are submerged in salt water.

Houses for hurricanes

Countries such as Jamaica and Australia have put strict building codes into place in hurricane zones. In Jamaica, corrugated iron roofs have to be tied down with hurricane straps. New buildings have to withstand 3-second gusts of wind at 125 miles (about 200 kilometers) per hour. In Australia, buildings less than 20 feet (about 6 meters) tall have to be able to cope with winds of up to 90 miles (about 150 kilometers) per hour.

Hurricanes cause a lot of economic problems when they hit poorer countries. This is partly because storms can ruin cash crops, which are often the main or only export. When exports are sold abroad, they bring in much-needed money.

Plant planning

Hurricanes can cause food shortages in poorer countries, but it is difficult to assess crop damage immediately after the disaster. The initial impact is obvious—fruit trees and tall-stemmed crops are broken and bent and leaves are ripped off. Some plants simply topple over, their roots loosened by floodwater and heavy rain. Others are smothered in mud and debris. Other, less obvious effects only emerge after time. These include rotted root crops and fruit trees that appear to have survived but which later do not bear fruit. This is because the blossoms and young fruit have been blown off by the wind. So what are the solutions?

Some of the answers are to plant specially-developed crops with shorter stems that will not break in the wind. Other solutions include planting crops that have a short growing season, so that they can be planted or harvested before the hurricane season. Planting more crops over a larger area increases the chances of a reasonable harvest, whatever the weather.

One way of not being hurt by hurricanes is to move out of danger. Belize's new capital city lies 50 miles (80 kilometers) inland. On October 31, 1961, the original city was flattened by Hurricane Hattie, and several hundred people were killed.

Why Live in Danger?

Millions of people in different parts of the world live in the paths of **hurricanes.** This is not because they do not realize the dangers, but because they have to make a living. Some of the world's most fertile regions like Bangladesh are situated on **floodplains** near river **estuaries.** In hurricane zones, these are also areas that are badly affected by **storm surges.** Coastal ports face the same problem. Many of these, too, are situated on estuaries, where goods can be transported downriver and shipped all over the world. River water is used in the manufacturing of wood products, chemicals, cloth, and many other goods, as well as in the cooling-towers of power stations. Many people enjoy living on the coast, with its beautiful scenery and fresh sea air.

The islands of Japan face **typhoons** from the western Pacific Ocean. These hit the eastern shores of Japan, where the country's largest cities are. This is because of the warm ocean current that runs along the coast. Warm waters fuel the hurricanes but, for the islanders, they also provide a better climate for agriculture. This, plus fishing, are what first attracted people to the east coast, where great cities have developed.

Cities at risk

Cities attract workers, and in much of the developing world huge numbers of poor farmers migrate to them to find wage-earning jobs. They build their homes on the edges, often on surrounding hills where there is a threat of mudslides. The houses are often badly built, and there are often no rules governing how they are constructed. **Sanitation** is poor. So in hurricane-prone cities in the developing world, a hurricane disaster causes a large loss of life and a lot of storm damage. Poor sanitation leads to a huge health hazard.

In all inner-city areas, space is very limited so buildings have to be tall. In most hurricane zones, new high-rise constructions have to comply with strict building regulations. These control construction methods and materials used for foundations, frames, and walls. Older buildings are very vulnerable to storm damage. Two kinds of hurricane wind threaten the city—a swirling **vortex** of winds bouncing around tall buildings, and the **Venturi effect,** where wind speed increases as it is channeled through narrow streets lined with high-rise buildings.

Beautiful beaches and hot, sunny weather have attracted millions of tourists to Miami Beach, Florida, which is right in the path of hurricanes.

In the United States, a lot of damage occurs in residential areas on the edges of cities. Newer block-built houses usually suffer a small amount of structural damage, but many people live in mobile homes or trailer parks, with lightweight trailers that are easily blown over by the winds.

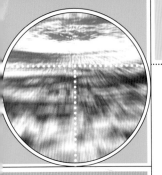

Hurricanes in History

Hurricanes have been around for a long time, as shown by stories of ancient storms. We know that weather conditions in small areas were recorded as long ago as the fourteenth century. Death tolls in the United States and Caribbean have been counted for over 300 years. But it is only in the last 100 years or so that governments and authorities have tried to assess the damage through pictures and eyewitness accounts.

It is only in the last 100 years, too, that we have tried to look at the causes of hurricanes in a methodical, scientific way. **Barometers** used for measuring **air pressure** have been around for centuries. So have weather vanes for locating the direction of the wind. But it is only in the last century that scientists have had the tools necessary to predict natural disasters. Tracking hurricanes using satellite images has only been made possible in the last 40 years—a relatively short time in scientific terms.

Galveston, Texas was hit by a hurricane in 1900. Over 12,000 people died. Most were drowned by a **storm surge.** It was the first disaster ever filmed, and it was shot by the famous inventor of the light bulb, Thomas Edison.

Historical hurricanes

There have been many deadly hurricanes since people started recording them, but we do not know if they were the most deadly hurricanes ever. Modern meteorology has allowed us to predict how often the worst hurricanes are likely to occur. From this we can work back in time and estimate what the damage might have been to communities of the past. One of the calculations made by modern **meteorologists** is how often hurricanes of various strengths occur. This way they can tell whether hurricanes have increased in number and intensity, and make educated guesses about the strength of historial hurricanes. Most meteorologists agree that hurricanes have not increased, but the damage they cause has.

Reports of deaths and damage from hurricanes in the past can give us information about how people lived. For example, hurricane-force winds hit England in 1703. At least 100 people were killed on land, but it is thought that probably 8,000 perished at sea. This tells us that there were many more fishermen and trading ships than there are today. Cities were much smaller and only increased during the industrial revolution that began about 80 years later. Throughout the world at that time, populations were smaller and more spread-out, so hurricane death tolls would probably not have been as great as they have been in the last 200 years.

Over 200 years ago, a hurricane hit the Lesser Antilles Islands in the Caribbean. Over 20,000 people died, making it the sixth worst hurricane in recorded history.

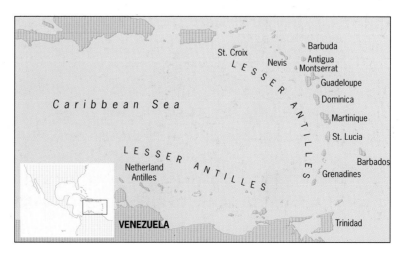

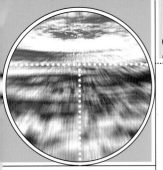

Taking Advantage—the Natural World

When **hurricanes** hit farmlands, cultivated plants bend, break, or rot in the soil. It is a similar story with farm animals. Animals in the wild might be able to sense a storm coming and be able to get out of the way. On a farm, though, they are often penned in with nowhere to go. Have plants and animals in the natural world adapted any better to hurricanes?

Along the west Atlantic coast, one of the first signs of an approaching hurricane is the sight of frigate birds swooping inland.

Warnings in West Africa

West Africa is often hit by hurricane-like conditions, just as the rainy season begins. We hear very little about these weather disasters because they rarely cause loss of life. However, they damage buildings and destroy crops and livestock. These conditions arise when the very warm, moist air from the Atlantic creates an area of **low pressure** that moves inland, towards the Sahara. Here, the climate is extremely hot and dry, creating a huge **high pressure** area that blows southward into the area of low pressure. The storms created by this **turbulence** affect the normally very dry Sahel and savannah regions. Here, natural plants have adapted to hurricane conditions. Tight clumps of grasses and short trees have strong spreading roots that cling tightly to the soil. Grass blades and shrubs sway in a rotating motion so they do not snap easily.

Animals, too, have developed ways of surviving and even taking advantage of tropical storms. Quelea birds, a type of weaver bird, weave colonies of rounded, protective nests attached to tree branches. Dozens of nests cling to the tree and sway unharmed with the branches as the wind rages.

Locusts also take advantage of the storms. Locust eggs are laid in the newly-wet soil, dampened by the rains that precede the storms. The eggs hatch in the warm, humid days that follow, then swarms of them are transported by high winds to feeding grounds all over West and North Africa. Here, the farmer loses out again, for the locusts eat everything green in sight— and even clothes hung out to dry!

Coral animals that build the reefs that protect the American coastlines **spawn,** or lay eggs, just before the onset of the hurricane season. These eggs float around the reef until the hurricane **storm surge** arrives, and the swaying seas transport the coral eggs over a wide area, where they begin life afresh.

The Storm is Coming

Birds in the rain forests of the Caribbean Islands build their weatherproof nests among the tall, wide trees that create a huge protective canopy over the forest floor. The trees are anchored well into the ground with massive, twisted root systems, so when the **hurricane** winds hit them they stand their ground. Leaves and twigs are ripped from branches that bend or snap, depending on how flexible they are. By this time, the birds have abandoned their nests and found cover on the forest floor. The heavy rains now reach through the broken canopy down onto the thin soil. The ground is soaked and the roots of the weakest rain forest trees loosen. High winds are still blowing and some trees finally fall. Some of the birds are lucky—their nests are left intact on the strongest trees. Others will quickly have to rebuild their nests before the mating season ends. But is it all bad news for the natural world?

Amphibians such as frogs and lizards are very sensitive to the sudden, deep drop in **air pressure** as a hurricane approaches. They call out for hours at a time until the hurricane arrives.

Winners and losers

Rain forest insects are now exposed to the light by the broken canopy and are eaten gratefully by hungry birds. But the hummingbird, which feeds on nectar, has to search hard for blossoms on the fallen trees. Thin-skinned amphibians are now exposed to the hot sun. But the fallen, broken tree trunks have provided pools of water for frogs to lay their eggs in.

These seabirds are taking advantage of extra fish and seafood brought to the surface by the hurricane.

After a few days, the humid air and the moist earth give just the right conditions for new trees to grow—especially species that get only a rare chance to push up between the thick trunks of the largest rain forest trees. Thinner-trunked trees such as the trumpet tree find their place in the forest.

When hurricanes move over the east coast of the United States, different habitats are hit. In the pine forests, woodpeckers are left homeless when the brittle trees where they had made their nests are toppled. Now they have to start all over again. But in the marshlands hit by a huge **storm surge,** alligators are unharmed. Their hard, earth nests lie untouched by the storm.

43

Amazing Hurricanes

The ten most deadly hurricanes in history

Place	Year	Number of deaths
Bangladesh	1970	Up to 500,000
Bangladesh	1991	131,000
Southeast India	1977	100,000
Bangladesh	1964	35,000
Northeast India and Bangladesh	1965	30,000
Lesser Antilles (Caribbean Sea)	1780	22,000
Bangladesh	1963	15,000
Bangladesh	1964	15,000
Galveston, Texas	1900	12,000
Bangladesh	1985	11,000

Breaking the bank

These are the five most costly **hurricanes** so far for the United States. The cost of Hurricane Georges is still being counted. Hurricanes cause more damage than any other natural disaster.

Date	Hurricane	Cost in millions of dollars
1992	Andrew	$15.5
1989	Hugo	$4.2
1992	Iniki	$1.6
1979	Frederic	$0.75
1983	Alicia	$0.68

The biggest weapon

Many of the deaths in the table opposite were caused by **storm surges,** the worst of which occur in India. They are frequent in the north around the Bay of Bengal, where **tropical cyclones** happen almost every year. Low-lying, highly-populated islands add to their impact. One of the deadliest storm surges in history hit the area southwest of Calcutta, India, in 1876. On its own, it is believed to have killed 100,000 people.

Naming hurricanes

Hurricanes are always given names, such as Hurricane Andrew or Hurricane Georges. This began over 100 years ago when an Australian **meteorologist** named Clement Wragge began identifying the storms using characters from mythology. He then moved on to politicians' names, which is when his system collapsed—the politicians did not like it! But the method of identification was renewed about 60 years ago and became the official system in 1952. At the beginning of the year, the first hurricane is given a name beginning with "A," the next, "B" and so on. They are given alternating male and female names.

The Netherlands were hit by a huge storm surge caused by hurricane force winds in 1953. Floods swept 40 miles (65 kilometers) inland and 2,000 people died. The disaster was so severe because a lot of the land lay below sea level. Since then, huge steel and concrete barriers have been built to keep out the waves. The one in the picture, at Neelje Jans, is also a park.

Glossary

air pressure amount of pressure put on the sea or land by the air

atmosphere layers of gases surrounding the earth

barometer instrument for measuring air pressure

carbon dioxide gas formed from carbon and oxygen that is given off when fossil fuels such as coal or oil are burned

condense to cool enough to turn from a gas into a liquid

Coriolis force effect of the earth's rotation on winds, making them curve

cumulonimbus heavy, rain-bearing type of cloud

deforestation large-scale cutting down of trees

delta new land formed by material deposited at the mouth of a river

Doppler radar system used to detect tornadoes that uses radio waves reflected off super-cooled water droplets or ice particles in thunderclouds

easterly jet surge of cold wind high up and from the east, at about 30,000 feet (10,000 meters) above the earth

El Niño periodic reversal of prevailing winds that causes climate change

equatorial near the equator

estuary very low-lying wet area where a river meets the sea

evacuate to move to safety

evaporate to heat enough to change from a liquid into a gas

flash flood sudden flood caused by torrential rainfall

floodplain low, flat area of land around where a river widens

fossil fuel fuel such as oil that comes from decayed plant or animal matter

front zone where high pressure areas and low pressure areas meet

global warming rise in the earth's temperature, possibly due to the emission of gases into the air

greenhouse effect warming effect caused by gases in the atmosphere trapping the heat from the sun

hemisphere half of the world north or south of the equator, or east or west of the Prime Meridian

high pressure area characterized by cool, dry air

hurricane tropical storm with winds of at least 75 miles (120 kilometers) per hour; also called typhoon or cyclone

hurricane warning late phase of hurricane warning, when evacuation plans are carried out

hurricane watch early phase of hurricane warning in the United States

Intertropical Convergence Zone (ITCZ) area around the equator where air is heated, rises, is dispersed, and then gets pulled back down towards the earth again

invested to put money into a project

landfall point at which a hurricane hits land

low pressure area characterized by warm, moist air

meteorologist scientist who studies the weather and climate

methane gas formed from decaying plant matter

millibar unit of measurement for atmospheric pressure

molecule smallest particle of a substance that has all its properties, usually made up of two or more atoms

monsoon winds winds that blow around the Indian Ocean, towards the southwest in the winter, and towards the north in the summer, when they bring rains and often hurricanes

oceanographer scientist who studies the sea and oceans

ozone form of oxygen that forms a layer around the earth, high in the atmosphere

polders land reclaimed from the sea for farming, often below sea level

radar system of reflecting high-powered radio pulses off objects to give an idea of their position and shape

radiate to send out rays of light or other energy

radiation energy given out by the sun or the earth

Saffir-Simpson hurricane scale scale that measures levels of hurricane damage and air pressure within hurricanes

sandblasting when wind blasts rough sand against buildings or structures, scouring away the surface

sanitation drainage systems for human and household waste and water

spawn to mate and lay eggs

storm surge huge wall of water formed when hurricane winds blow over the ocean and pile up the water

stratosphere layer of the atmosphere above the troposphere

super-cooled cooled below the freezing point, but not yet turned to ice. When super-cooled water touches something else, even a particle of dust, it will immediately freeze.

tornado violent, twisting, sucking wind that rotates around a funnel of very low air pressure

tropical cyclone technical name for a hurricane, used in Australia and India

tropopause layer of the atmosphere between the troposphere and the stratosphere

troposphere layer of the atmosphere closest to the earth

turbulence condition of the air characterized by choppy, rapid movement of masses of air

typhoon name given to hurricanes around the western Pacific, China, and the islands of Japan

ultra-violet rays light from the sun that falls outside the range of visible wavelengths

Venturi effect effect of wind being channeled through narrow city streets lined with high-rise buildings and becoming stronger

vortex fast twisting funnel

water cycle process by which water is continually recycled in different forms

water vapor water in its gaseous state

More Books to Read

Buckley, James. *Hurricane and Tornado.* New York: DK Publishing, 2000.

Green, Jen. *Hurricanes and Typhoons.* Brookfield, Conn.: Millbrook Press, Inc., 1998.

Meister, Cari. *Hurricanes.* Minneapolis, Minn.: ABDO Publishing Co., 1999.

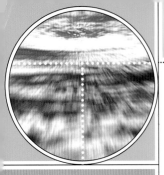

Index